JOHN DRYDEN

THE POET

THE DRAMATIST

THE CRITIC

Three Essays by T. S. ELIOT

HASKELL HOUSE
Publishers of Scholarly Books
NEW YORK
1966

First Published 1932

HASKELL HOUSE PUBLISHERS LTD.
Publishers of Scarce Scholarly Books
280 LAFAYETTE STREET
NEW YORK, N. Y. 10012

Library of Congress Catalog Card Number: **68-913**

Standard Book Number 8383-0692-6

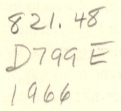

Printed in the United States of America

RYDEN's position in English literature is unique. Far below Shakespeare, and even below Milton, as we must put him, he yet has, just by reason of his precise degree of inferiority, a kind of importance which neither Shakespeare nor Milton has—the importance of his *influence*. It is this nice question of influence that I wish to investigate first, in relation to what I may call the "literary dictator," that is, in our history, Ben Jonson, Dryden, Samuel Johnson and in his way, Coleridge. Are we to say that poets like Shakespeare and Milton were without influence? Certainly not, but "influence," in the sense in which we can cope with the term, is something more limited. The disproportion between Shakespeare and his immediate followers, among the dramatists, is so great that the influence of Shakespeare is a trifling

thing in comparison with Shakespeare himself;

and as for Milton, that was so peculiar a genius that although he had plenty of mimics during the eighteenth century, he can hardly be said to have any followers. For "influence," as Dryden had influence, a poet must not be so great as to overshadow all followers. Dryden was followed by Pope, and a century later, by Samuel Johnson; both men of great original genius, who developed the medium left them by Dryden, in ways which cast honour both on them and on him. It should seem then no paradox to say that Dryden was the great influence upon English verse that he was, because he was *not* too great to have any influence at all. He was neither the consummate poet of earlier times, nor the eccentric poet of later. He was happy both in his predecessors and in his successors. A hundred years is a long time for the stamp of one man to remain upon a literature; poets' influence and reputation cannot last so long in our days; and that makes Dryden a central, a typical figure in English letters. He is in himself the Malherbe, the Boileau, the Corneille and almost the Molière (almost, because Congreve refined and surpassed him in comedy) of the seventeenth century in England; and to him, as much as to any individual, we owe our civilisation.

As a figure, there is nothing picturesque about the man John Dryden. He came of a small county family like hundreds of others; he had, for a man of his origins, no great worldly advantages; he married a lady of superior rank, who brought him no exceptional advantage either, and apparently little domestic happiness. He was an ordinary seeming, florid countryman, whose manners, according to the next and more refined generation, were not of the most polished. We do not know whether it was by the brilliance of his conversation that he was the great figure of Wills's Coffee House for all the hours that he passed there every day; but there he was, admired by minor men of letters, and courted by bluestocking noblemen. If not because of his powers of talk, in an age when men *John* talked and drank for more hours a day than *Dryden* they can afford to do now, and when they wrote, wrote at higher speed than we can, then it was because they all recognised that Dryden could do everything that they would have liked to do, and because what he wrote did not exceed the scope of their comprehension. I cannot imagine Shakespeare cutting such a figure in a tavern or coffee-house; that solitary person surely had too much in his head which his taproom companions could not understand; the predecessor of Dryden in this role is, of course, Ben Jonson. But although of Jonson we have so few personal remains, yet the notes and the anecdotes which we have give us at least the illusion of as definite a character as that of Dr. Samuel Johnson. We remember the story of Ben Jonson, that when he returned to the Anglican fold after his temporary defection to Rome, he showed his enthusiasm by seizing the 8 chalice, at his first communion, and draining it to the last drop. We can never see Dryden so clearly; yet his age was in accord that he ex- *The* pressed each man better than any man could *Poet* express himself.

Being so completely representative, Dryden not only formed the mould for the next age, but himself derived very clearly from the last. In his work there is nothing unexpected, no new element with unknown properties. As a poet, Dryden came to resolve the contradictions of the previous period, and select from it the styles which were capable of development. His first verse, though clever enough of its kind to earn ready commendations, is distinctly bad. It is encumbered with all the late metaphysical conceits which he was himself to destroy. Cleveland and Benlowes are lightfooted by comparison; for they traced their patterns with conviction; and of the early verses of Dryden one can only say that they are by a man doing his best to talk an idiom alien to him: but for sudden flashes of wit and sense here and there, one

would say that their author could never be a
poet. It used to be thought that the poetic styles
of Dryden and Pope were artificial. One has
only to compare them with the style of Dryden's
immediate predecessor, Abraham Cowley, to
prove the contrary. Dryden became a great poet
because he could *not* write an artificial style;
because it was intolerable to him; because he
had that uncorruptible sincerity of word which
at all times distinguishes the good writer from
the bad, and at critical times such as his, distinguishes the great writer from the little one. What
Dryden did in fact was to reform the language,
and devise a natural, conversational style of
speech in verse in place of an artificial and de-
cadent one.

Too much can still be made, I think, of
Dryden's debt to Waller and Denham, and to
his contemporary Oldham. Oldham, certainly,
is very near to him; Oldham is rough and un-
polished, but occasionally in his "rugged line"
10 there breaks out a vigour not unlike Dryden's.

His satires are still readable. But to Waller and Denham, as practitioners of the heroic couplet, *The Poet* his debt can be exaggerated. As Pope says, "Waller was smooth," indeed, but his smoothness is feebleness, compared to anything accomplished by Dryden or Pope himself: the smoothness of an ambling pad-pony compared to that of a fiery horse with an expert rider. Waller mostly, and Denham except in one passage, send us to sleep; and Dryden never allows us to do that. I think that Dryden owes more to his reaction against the artifices of the late metaphysical verse, than to any sedulous study of Waller. For the content of his couplet, the sensibility which informs it, is as different from that of Waller as well could be.

It is not irrelevant to compare the operation of Dryden with that of Donne. Donne likewise was a reformer of the language. This is not so immediately apparent in Donne's case, for his career is overlapped by the Elizabethan dramatists, who were still, after Shakespeare, exploring the possibilities of dramatic blank verse. John Dryden But consider that Shakespearean blank verse was soon to expire with the set phrases of Shirley and others, that it had nearly gone its course, and consider what the lyric verse of Shakespeare's time was. It was essentially verse for music; therefore its intellectual content and its range of emotion were restricted. The songs of Shakespeare gain a great deal—perhaps this has not been enough remarked—by their dramatic position in the plays: a song like "full fathom five" is suffused by the meaning and feeling of the passage in which it occurs; the songs of Shakespeare are not interludes or interruptions, but part of the structure of the plays in which they occur. Observing this attribute, we can say that for lyric verse there was very little future, had it not been for Donne. Donne did away with all the stage properties of the ordinary lyric verse of the Elizabethans; he introduced into lyric verse a style of conversation, of direct natural speech; and this was a revolution comparable to the development of blank verse into a conversational medium, from Kyd to the ma- ture Shakespeare. And by this innovation Donne gave to the Caroline poets a vehicle which they would hardly have been able to devise for themselves.

By the time when Dryden began to write, the vigour of the style initiated by Donne had quite gone: the natural had become the artificial. For there is not, in verse, any wholly objective distinction between the natural and the artificial style. Whether a style is natural is whether it is natural to the man who writes it. It is harder to be natural than to be artificial, it requires a great deal more work, and is painful and unpleasant, because sincerity is always painful and unpleasant. Well, Dryden did the work, and experienced no doubt the pain and unpleasantness, and he restored English verse to the condition of speech.

Now when we say "conversational," or the quality of the spoken language in verse, we are inclined to limit it to certain kinds of conversation, perhaps more particularly of an intimate nature; so it is easier for us to perceive this naturalness in Donne than in Dryden. But we have to consider what are the essentials of good speech. At no time, I know, are the written language and the spoken language identical. Obviously, they cannot be: if we talked extempore exactly as we write, no one would listen, and if we wrote exactly as we talk, no one would read. But speech can never divorce itself, beyond some point, from the written word, without damage to itself; and writing can never beyond some point alienate itself from speech, without self-destruction. Now Dryden's couplets may not seem at first sight to echo our own way of speech. That may be partly because the standards of good English in conversation were higher then, and partly because the spoken word, in the late seventeenth and eighteenth centuries, meant much more *public* speech than it does to us; it meant oratory and eloquence.

True, thanks to the radio, we more often listen to public oratory than we did a few years ago. But we hardly expect the sublime; we may prefer the chatty, and if any of our acquaintance, in private company, holds forth and harangues at length, we are apt to qualify him as a bore. But, in the time of Dryden, speech was rather speech in public than in private; and Dryden helped to form a language for generations which were prepared to speak, and to listen, in public.

There are of course three main divisions of Dryden's verse, apart from the verse of the heroic plays: the satires, the songs, and the translations. Now one of the good offices of Dryden in his satires is this: to show us that if verse should not stray too far from the customs of speech, so also it should not abandon too much the uses of prose. Everyone knows the verses of *Mac Flecknoe* and the more varied if less sustained satire of *Absalom and Achitophel*; I should like here to mention rather those two pieces of sustained reasoning in verse, *Religio Laici* and *The Hind and the Panther*. Here are two poems which could no more have been written in the eighteenth century than in the nineteenth, for they are poems of religious controversy. Other poets, before Dryden, had, in divers fashions, philosophised in verse: Chapman, and Sir John Davies, and Donne, in his way, in *The Progress of the Soul*. But in *The Hind and the Panther* for the first time and for the last is political-religious controversy elevated to the condition of poetry. However one views these differences now, one cannot but appreciate the characterisation of the Church of England, under the guise of the Panther, which Dryden draws, after his conversion to Rome:

Thus, like a creature of a double kind,
In her own labyrinth she lives confined.
To foreign lands no sound of her is come,
Humbly content to be despised at home.
Such is her faith, where good cannot be had,
16 *At least she leaves the refuse of the bad.*

Nice in her choice of ill, though not of best,
And least deform'd, because reform'd the least ... The
A real presence all her sons allow, Poet
And yet 'tis flat idolatry to bow,
Because the Godhead's there, they know not how ...
What is't those faithful then partake or leave?
For what is signified and understood,
Is, by her own confession, flesh and blood.
Then, by the same acknowledgement, we know
They take the sign, and take the substance too.
The lit'ral sense is hard to flesh and blood.
But nonsense never can be understood.

This is not, when analysed, convincing theological argument—Dryden was no theologian
—but it is first-rate oratorical persuasion; and
Dryden was the first man to raise oratory to
the dignity of poetry, and to descend with poetry to teach the arts of oratory; and to do any
one thing with verse better than anyone else
has done it, at the same time that one is the
first to attempt it, is no small achievement. But
it is not only by biting passages like this that *17*

a poem of Dryden's succeeds, but by a perfect lifting and lowering of his flight, in a varied unity without monotony. Take the beginning of the earlier and inferior of the two poems, *Religio Laici,* the passage attacking the principles of deism:

> *Dim as the borrowed beams of moon and stars*
> *To lonely, weary, wandering travellers*
> *Is Reason to the soul: and as on high*
> *Those rolling fires discover but the sky,*
> *Not light us here, so Reason's glimmering ray*
> *Was lent, not to assure our doubtful way*
> *But guide us upward to a better day.*
> *And as those nightly tapers disappear*
> *When day's bright lord ascends our hemisphere,*
> *So pale grows Reason at Religion's sight,*
> *So dies, and so dissolves in supernatural light.*

This, if I am not greatly mistaken, is first-rate poetry not incomparable to Lucretius—of whom, by the way, Dryden by a few passages proved himself the most worthy translator into

English of any time. And the same vein is re-
peated, with still greater power, in *The Hind*
and the Panther:

But, gracious God, how well dost thou provide
For erring judgements an unerring guide!
Thy throne is darkness in the abyss of light,
A blaze of glory that forbids the sight.
O teach me to believe Thee thus concealed,
And search no farther than Thyself revealed;
But her alone for my director take,
Whom Thou hast promised never to forsake!
My thoughtless youth was winged with vain
   desires;
My manhood, long mislead by wandering fires,
Followed false lights; and when their glimpse was
   gone,
My pride struck out new sparkles of her own.
Such was I, such by nature still I am;
Be Thine the glory, and be mine the shame!

Anyone who to-day could make such an exact
statement in verse of such nobility and elegance,

and with such originality of versification and
language, might well look down upon his contemporaries. We are very far, here, from the
smoothness of Waller or Denham. The surface
is equally polished; but the difference is between
the smooth surface of a piece of sculpture con-
ceived and finished by a master and the smooth
surface of a cake of soap.

I shall have occasion to refer again to Dryden's verse translations, including his translations from Chaucer, in connection with his literary criticism. I will only say here that they
are more or less satisfactory, naturally, according to Dryden's sympathy with the original,
and that perhaps his translations from Lucretius
are the most inspired. All are of the best workmanship. Their importance, however, in considering Dryden's place then and now, is this:
that it was by his translations almost as much
as by his original poems, that Dryden helped
to form our modern English tongue. It is no
inconsiderable service to a language, to dem-

onstrate that great poetry of other languages and times can be translated into the speech which we use daily, and remain great poetry. It might be a good thing for the language to-day if living poets would devote more attention to translating poetry from both living languages and dead; for the language at Dryden's time it was of vital assistance. Nor shall I now say much about, or quote from, Dryden's lyrical verse. Whatever we think of the *Song for St. Cecilia's Day* or of *Alexander's Feast* we must remember that in these Dryden perfected a form used with less skill by Cowley, and bequeathed it to Gray, Collins, Wordsworth, Coleridge and Tennyson; and without Dryden the *Intimations of Immortality* could not have been written.

The main point, which I wish to drive home about Dryden is this: that it was Dryden who for the first time, and so far as we are concerned, for all time, established a *normal* English speech, a speech valid for both verse and prose, and imposing its laws which greater poetry than

Dryden's might violate, but which no poetry since has overthrown. The English language as left by Shakespeare, and within much narrower limits, by Milton, was a language like the club of Hercules, which no lesser strength could wield; so I believe that the language after Shakespeare and Milton could only have deteriorated until some genius appeared as great as they—or indeed, greater than they: for the language would have been quickly in far worse case than that in which Shakespeare found it. It was Dryden, more than any other individual, who formed a language possible for the mediocrity, and yet possible for later great writers to do great things with.

And what Dryden accomplished was no by-product and no accident. Never was there a worker more conscious of what he was attempting. His theories, as we shall see, were all theories directed to what the poet could *consciously* attempt. Coleridge, in his writings on poetry, far exceeds the limited flight of Dryden, and disappears in metaphysic clouds. The theory of Coleridge is partly, certainly, as was that of Wordsworth, a defence of his conscious precepts of workmanship; but with Wordsworth, and still more with Coleridge, we can say that their theory does not wholly account for the best of their poetry. In this way, Dryden was a far more *conscious* poet than either; perhaps more conscious than any poet of great eminence since. His essays are his conscious thoughts about the kinds of work he was doing; he uttered no metaphysical speculations, he was no prophet or teacher. I can think of no man in literature whose aims are so exactly fulfilled by his performance; and in the whole vineyard no labourer who more deserved his hire.

So I think now that we can understand a little better why John Dryden, of whose personality we know little, except to know that there was little that was romantic or eccentric about it, should have dominated his time. Even if this portly country gentleman had sat hour

after hour at Wills's, as silent as Addison's de-
scription of himself as Mr. Spectator, it is perfectly intelligible. It is hardly too much to say
that Dryden found the English speechless, and
he gave them speech; and they accordingly
acknowledged their master; the language which
we can refine, enrich, distort or corrupt as we
may, but which we cannot do without. No one,
in the whole history of English literature, has
dominated that literature so long, or so completely. And even in the nineteenth century the
language was still the language of Dryden, as
it is to-day. In two hundred odd years, or exactly three hundred years from his birth, hardly
a word or a phrase has become quaint and ob-
solete. And yet the man who accomplished so
much, and accomplished it so consciously, was
content to do whatever came to hand; and for
twenty years of his life occupied himself exclu-
sively in order to make his living with a form
of literature to which his talent was little suited,
and that form too he transformed.

Dryden the Dramatist

IT is not such an easy matter to explain the utility to English letters and civilisation of Dryden's dramatic work, as it is to persuade of the importance of his poetry. Here are, in the edition of 1735 which I have, six volumes of miscellaneous plays, the chief product of twenty years of his life: it would be in a modern edition a fairly stout volume. The point is: are we to consider these plays as merely the by-product or waste-product of a man of genius, or as the brilliant effort to establish an impossible cause, or have they, perhaps, any important relation to the development of English literature? Would Dryden be as important as he is, would he have accomplished just as much as he did, if he had never written these plays at all; plays, one or two of which a small number of people to-day have had the opportunity of seeing on the stage, and three or four of which a rather larger number of people have read?

We begin, all of us, with every prejudice John against Dryden's "heroic drama." There is one Dryden great play in blank verse, *All for Love*, and the difficulty about that is that Shakespeare's play on the same subject, *Antony and Cleopatra*, is very much greater—though not necessarily a much finer *play*. There are several fine plays in rhymed couplets, of which there is none better than *The Conquest of Granada*, and the trouble with them is that they are not in blank verse. It is extraordinarily difficult not to apply to these plays irrelevant standards of criticism, and standards, moreover, which are not exactly of play-writing or even of verse-making. We have always at the back of our minds a comparison which is not in kind. Most of us prefer the reading, not only of Shakespeare, but of several other Elizabethan dramatists to that of Dryden. And in our reading of Elizabethan plays, we are inclined to confer upon them the dramatic virtues of the most actable (on the modern stage) of Shakespeare's plays, because they have some of the *reading*

28

virtues of these and the rest of Shakespeare's plays. I shall not venture here to investigate the nature of the *dramatic* in poetic drama, as distinguishable from the *poetic* in poetic drama; only to point out that the problem is much more of a tangle than it looks. For instance, there is *that which expressed in word and action is effective on the stage without our having read the text before:* that might be called the *theatrically dramatic;* and there is also the "poetically dramatic," that which, when we read it, we recognize to have dramatic value, but which would not have dramatic value for us upon the stage unless we had already the perception of it from reading. *Theatrically* dramatic value in verse exists when the speech has its equivalent in, or can be projected by, the action and gesture and expression of the actor; *poetic* dramatic value is something dramatic in essence which can only be expressed by the word and by the reception of the word.

Shakespeare, of course, made the utmost use of each value; and therefore confuses us in our at-

tempt to estimate between the minor Elizabethans and Dryden, for neither they nor Dryden
had such vast resources. But to make my point
a little clearer I will take parallel passages from
Antony and Cleopatra and from *All for Love*. In
the former play, when the soldiers burst in after
Cleopatra's death Charmian is made to say

> *It is well done, and fitting for a princess*
> *Descended of so many royal kings.*
> *Ah, soldier!* (dies).

Dryden's Charmion says

> *Yes, 'tis well done, and like a Queen, the last*
> *Of her great race. I follow her.*
> *(Sinks down and dies).*

Now, if you take these two passages by themselves, you cannot say that the two lines of Dryden are either less *poetic* than Shakespeare's, or
less *dramatic*; a great actress could make just as
much, I believe, of those of Dryden as of those
of Shakespeare. But consider Shakespeare's re-

markable addition to the original text of North, the two plain words *ah, soldier*. You cannot say that there is anything peculiarly *poetic* about these two words, and if you isolate the dramatic from the poetic, you cannot say that there is anything peculiarly dramatic either, because there is nothing in them for the actress to express in action; she can at best enunciate them clearly. I could not myself put into words the difference I feel between the passage if these two words *ah, soldier* were omitted and with them. But I know there is a difference, and that only Shakespeare could have made it.

One might say that Dryden was a great poet who, by close application of a first rate mind, made himself a great dramatist. His best plays are a happy marriage, or a happy compromise, between poetry and drama. You cannot say, when he is at his best, that he is less dramatic than Shakespeare, often he is more *purely* dramatic; nor can you say that he is less poetic. It is merely that there is a flight above, at which poetry and drama become one thing; of which *John* one is often reminded in passages of Homer or *Dryden* Dante. We often feel with Shakespeare, and now and then with his lesser contemporaries, that the dramatic action on the stage is the symbol and shadow of some more serious action in a world of feeling more real than ours, just as our perceptions, in dreams, are often more ominously weighted than they are in practical waking life. As Chapman says

That all things to be done, as here we live,
Are done before all times in the other life.

Here again is a passage, from the dying words of a hero of Chapman, which I will contrast presently with words of a hero of Dryden.

Here like a Roman statue I will stand
Till death hath made me marble; oh, my fame,
Live in despite of murder; take thy wings
And haste thee where the grey-eyed morn perfumes
Her rosy chariot with Sabæan spices,
32 Fly, where the evening from the Iberian vales

Takes on her swarthy shoulders Hecate
Crowned with a grove of oaks: fly where men feel   The
The cunning axle-tree: and those that suffer   Dramatist
Beneath the chariot of the snowy Bear:
And tell them all that D'Ambois now is hasting
To the eternal dwellers.

Here is an equally well known purple passage
from *All for Love*.

How I loved
Witness ye Days and nights, and all ye hours.
That danced away with down upon your feet,
As all your business were to count my passion.
One day passed by, and nothing saw but love,
Another came, and still 'twas only love,
The suns were wearied out with looking on,
And I untired with loving.
I saw you every day, and all the day;
And every day was still but as the first:
So eager was I still to see you more . . . .
        While within your arms I lay,
The world fell mouldering from my hands each hour   *33*

And left me scarce a grasp....

John   *.... I knew not that I fled;*

Dryden *But fled to follow you.*

    —What haste she made to hoist her purple sails!

Now, you cannot say that one of these passages, that of Chapman or that of Dryden, is more purple than the other, or better poetry. Both are inferior in that each does to excess one part of what Shakespeare can do. Chapman departs too far from the direct stage action into the second world which the visual symbolises; Dryden is also excessively poetic, or rather too consciously poetic, by lavishing such fine poetry *solely* in the direct action. Chapman has only overtone; and Dryden has none. But if you consider the lines of Dryden solely as poetry, or solely as drama, you cannot find a flaw in them.

As for the verse of *All for Love* and the best of Dryden's blank verse in the other plays in which he used it, it is to me a miracle of revivification. I think that it has more influence than

it has had credit for; and that it is really the norm of blank verse for later blank verse play- *The*
wrights. How Dryden could have escaped so *Dramatist* completely the bad influence of the last follow-ers of Shakespeare, with their dissolution of rhythm nearly into prose, and their wornout wardrobe of imagery, is as wonderful as his superiority to, and difference from the other schools of verse, that of the Senecal poets, and D'Avenant to whom he was somewhat in-debted. I will hazard here an heretical and con-testable opinion: that later blank verse drama-tists have written better verse when they wrote more like Dryden, and worse blank verse when they were conscious of Shakespeare. When Shel-ley wrote in *The Cenci*

My God! Can it be possible I have
To die so suddenly? So young to go
Under the obscure, cold, rotting, wormy ground!
To be nailed down into a narrow place;
To see no more sweet sunshine . . . .

I feel that this was not worth doing, because it
is only a feeble echo of the tremendous speech
of Claudio in *Measure for Measure*; but Shelley
is not the only poet who has been Shakespearean by the appropriation of worms and rot and
such Elizabethan stage properties. But other
lines, such as

> *worse than despair,*
> *Worse than the bitterness of death, is hope:*
> *It is the only ill which can find place*
> *Upon the giddy, sharp and narrow hour*
> *Tottering beneath us*

are more, in their context, like Dryden—though
in *The Cenci* resemblances are confused by the
nature of the subject, which is more sympathetic
to Ford than to either Shakespeare or Dryden.
And much more obviously than in the play of
Shelley—which I have chosen for mention because it is obviously of Elizabethan model—
is the debt to Dryden present in the plays of
Byron.

The skill of Dryden's blank verse is all the more admirable when one admits that it is a tour de force: blank verse is not natural to him. We shall see that in one of his critical essays he presents a most able defence of the rhymed couplet in heroic drama; but I always feel that here Dryden founded his reasons for what he believed upon instinct. Just as he had to defend the heroic drama because it happened to be the only form possible for the time, so I suspect that he defended the rhymed couplet because it was the form of verse which came most natural to him. There is not a line in *All for Love* which has, to my ear, the conversational tone of the best of Dryden's satires. As he adapted himself to drama, so he had, as far as possible, to adapt the drama to himself. Not that he was the first or the last to rhyme on the stage. But there is no other poet to whom the couplet came so naturally as the vehicle of speech as it did to Dryden; what he did not do with it cannot be done; and his couplet, miraculously,

is speech. There are two reasons for the com-
parative success of his rhyming in drama: first, he regularly relaxed the phrasing and made his lines run on as much as possible, so that they are technically different from his satire, and though still closely packed, less compressed; and of course he helps himself out with broken lines and triplets. The other reason is that he limits himself to those dramatic effects for which the rhymed couplet is adequate. Now the kind of play that he tried to write, and succeeded in writing, was a kind which would have been in existence, whether Dryden had written or not; and as it was there, it is wholly a merit on the part of Dryden to have written that kind of play in rhymed verse. The rhymed plays, such as *The Conquest of Granada* and *Au-rung-Zebe*, would *not* have been such good plays as they are, had they been written in blank verse, even blank verse as good as Dryden's. So that Dryden himself, in defending rhyme in the drama, oversimplifies the problem: for as a

We must call Dryden's plays "heroic drama" because we certainly can not call them tragedy. Even though he kills people off at the end, and though a dying queen raves in couplets better than one would conceive it possible for rhymed couplets to rave, what Dryden has is not the sense of tragedy at all. Indeed, it is from one point of view ironic to call these plays even "heroic"; for though he does not introduce the comic scene, some of his most effective passages are in a tone of witty satire, and are those in which the protagonists appear least heroic. For Dryden is an observer of human nature, rather than a creator.

I suspect that when Dryden regretted his efforts in comedy he was not merely deploring their licentiousness, which seems pretty innocent fun nowadays, but less consciously admitting their defects. Everything else that Dryden attempted, he brought to perfection in its kind, but in comedy he is a crude precursor of Congreve, and less admirable than Wycherley at his

best. His is the Restoration world, certainly,
John not that of the simple Elizabethan humours; but
Dryden his most polished figures of comedy, are, compared to the finest Restoration comedy, almost bumpkins; that delightful lady of *Marriage à la Mode*, Melantha, is still too "humorous" in her French affectations; and the fun of *Mr. Limberham* is not altogether well-bred. What I think is most noticeable, however, is that in his comedies Dryden was not able to bring his prose to perfection; it is a transition prose; and I doubt anyway whether his heart was in it. Dryden was quick enough to recognise the real right thing in prose dialogue; when young Mr. Congreve came along no one extolled him more highly than the older master of English letters. Congreve's prose is truly what we ordinarily call poetic; at any rate, I believe that the only two dramatists who have ever attained perfect prose in comedy—meaning perfect prose *for* comedy, are Shakespeare and Congreve.

42 But Dryden was not *naturally* a dramatist,

as Shakespeare and Congreve were natural dramatists. His direct service to English drama is— *The
apart from the value of his plays themselves— *Dramatist*
but here I am estimating the obligation of later
times to Dryden, and not Dryden himself—his
direct service is largely negative: had he not developed his own form of heroic play, which was
suited to, and representative of his time, it is
likely that a more and more etiolated Jacobean-
ism, with decayed versification, would have lin-
gered on. His great service to the drama is merely
incidental to his service to English letters.

We are apt to think, for convenience, and to
forget that it is merely a convenience, of the
development of prose and the development of
verse as two parallel currents which never mingle.
But Dryden's verse, for example, affects the history of English prose almost as much as his prose
does. I have suggested that it is a bad sign when
the written language and the spoken language
drift too far apart. It is also bad when poetry
and prose are too far apart; certainly, a poet *43*

can learn essential knowledge from the study of *John* the best prose, and a prose writer can learn from *Dryden* the study of the best verse; for there are problems of expression common to both. But for Dryden's verse, we might not have had the perfection of Congreve's prose: though this is not demonstrable. Prose which has *nothing* in common with verse is dead; verse which has nothing in common with prose is probably artificial, false, diffuse, and syntactically weak. We commonly find versifiers who are prosaic, and prose writers who dress out their flat writing with withered flowers of poetic rhetoric, and this is just the opposite of what I have in mind. I do not believe that in any modern civilisation prose can flourish if all the verse being written is bad, or that good verse can be written in an atmosphere choked with bad prose. If I am right, the beneficent influence of Dryden's poetry cannot be confined to those poets his disciples, but is diffused over the whole of English thought and *44* expression.

I cannot, finally, pretend to demonstrate that Dryden had a beneficent influence on English tragic drama—but only for the reason that since Dryden there has been no English tragic drama to influence. I have tried to affirm a belief, at least, that Dryden's dramatic work has, besides the pleasure it can give us for its merits unique in English literature, importance in the following ways: first, I believe that it strengthened his command of his verse medium for other work, and enlarged his interests; then, because of its interest for his own time, and because of the importance of the theatre in his time, it helped to consolidate his influence upon his contemporaries and successors; it is an essential member of the body of his work, which must be taken as a whole; and lastly, because it gave him the knowledge and the opportunity for some of his best critical writing—which last, as I shall try to show, has been of enduring value.

DRYDEN THE CRITIC

Dryden the Critic

THE prose writings of Dryden, whether in the standard edition of W. P. Ker, or in the convenient "Everyman" edition, consist entirely of prefaces to various volumes of verse or of verse plays. For the most part, they are concerned either with his views on poetic drama, or with his views on the art of translation. They are occasional, and constitute a kind of commentary on what he was doing in verse; they are the notes of a practitioner. They are obviously important in two ways: in the history of the development of English prose style, and in the history of English criticism; they are of further importance to us here, in reckoning the importance of the whole work of Dryden; for they form a part of this whole work which cannot be neglected.

Dryden's Essays are first, important in the history of English prose. As I have said, Dryden's verse exercised the most vital influence on

English poetry for nearly a century; similarly, *John* his prose had a temporary, and has a permanent, *Dryden* value for English critical prose style; but the great influence of Dryden cannot be divided into two currents; his main influence was upon the matter of thought and feeling out of which both verse and prose are made; his own verse and prose can therefore not be wholly separated, though we may say that he probably influenced prose by his verse still more than by his prose. I mean, that if we consider him as a writer of critical prose alone, we cannot say that his influence was dominant. We find similar tendencies in style in other contemporary writers on other subjects; and no one could go so far as to maintain that but for Dryden, we should have had neither the essays of Addison nor the writings of Swift at the point of perfection which these two writers reached. One can more plausibly conjecture, that but for the criticism of Dryden, we might not have Addison's critical *50* essays on Milton or on the ballads; for Dryden

was positively the first master of English criticism; and he set a good example for critics by
practising what he preached.

In Dryden's prose style, we find no such painful development as we find in his verse. His
prose seems to spring spontaneously, perfectly
modelled. There is nothing surprising about
this; it would be surprising if Dryden had not
written good prose. Anyone who has studied
his poetry, from his crude beginnings to his
perfect accomplishment, must be aware that
Dryden was gradually acquiring those elements
of good writing which are fundamental to both
verse and prose, whilst he was freeing himself
from the artificial poeticality of the previous
age. His training in verse was training in prose
as well; so that when, in maturity, he set himself, after the example of Corneille, to writing
critical introductions to his own verse, his prose
style is perfectly finished—indeed, larger and
more supple than the prose style of Corneille
himself. I have conceded that Dryden's prose

is only one of the prose styles of his time that *John* went to the formation of our form of classic *Dryden* English prose; but among these styles it is certainly one of the most admirable. He has all the virtues you would expect. He neither descends too low, nor attempts to fly too high; he is perfectly clear as to what he has to say; and he says it always with the right control and changes of intensity of feeling. His wit exceeds that of all his contemporaries; it contributes elegance and liveliness of figure, without ever overreaching itself into facetiousness. He has not the passion of his cousin Swift; but he everywhere convinces us of the serious, singleminded integrity of his love of truth in poetry, and his contempt for shams; and no writer in the next and more polished generation, not even Addison, has more urbanity. "Elegance" and "urbanity"; two words of commendation which have long been in disrepute; but which are always needed.

I know of no finer example of the precision and also of the range of Dryden's prose style, than the essay which we usually read first: the *Essay of Dramatic Poesy*. It may seem an ab- surd and unjust comparison, but I can think of no essay in dialogue form in English, which on its own plane—less sublime, less profound in thought—compares more favourably with some of the dialogues of Plato: it reminds me at the beginning particularly of the beautiful introduction to the *Theætetus*. "It was that memorable day, in the first summer of the late war, when our navy engaged the Dutch." No one who has ever read it can forget the undertone of naval cannonading above which are raised the voices of Eugenius, Crites, Neander and Lisideius, as they discuss in their barge on the river the various practices of Greek, French and English drama, the merits of the several tragic writers, and the claims of blank and rhymed verse. And here, and in all his prose, Dryden is, as in his verse, in perfect training; there is nowhere an ounce of superfluous fat; he is neither anæmic nor apoplectic; every blow delivered has just the right force

The
Critic

53

behind it. When we read such memorable phrases *John Dryden* as these from his essay *Examen Poeticum*:

> *"The same parts and application which have made me a poet might have raised me to any honours of the gown, which are often given to men of as little learning and less honesty than myself. No Government has ever been, or ever can be, wherein time-servers and blockheads will not be uppermost. The persons are only changed, but the same jugglings in State, the same hypocrisy in religion, the same self-interest and mismanagement, will remain for ever. Blood and money will be lavished in all ages only for the preferment of new faces and old consciences."*

Who, reading such passages, cannot understand at once that they should be by the author of Absalom and Achitophel, and who could doubt that their author, had he set himself the task, might have been one of the greatest of political orators?

But to turn from the manner to the matter 54 of these prefaces, we observe first that they are the first serious literary criticism in English by an English poet. We cannot quite say the first serious criticism, because there is for instance the contemporary criticism of Thomas Rymer —a critic of whom Dryden speaks highly, and of whom I should be tempted to speak more highly still. But Dryden was the first poet to theorise, on any large scale, about his own craft. I say on any large scale. There had been criticism in the previous age; but the only one I know, which has any precise and permanent value, is the admirable short treatise of Campion on metre and quantity—unless one except the reply to it by Daniel, and the graceful but ineffectual skirmishing of Philip Sidney. Dryden had, certainly, the example of the prefaces of Corneille in French, to which he was clearly indebted. But Dryden has proved a more important critic for the English language than was Corneille for the French. Rapin and Bossu, to whom Dryden refers, were more important in France than their colleagues in England; it is possible that France has had too many critics of poetry who could not practise it, and England too many poets who were not self-critical; but in Dryden we have, considering his limitation by his own time, an almost ideal balance between the critic and the creative poet.

And as for his limitations of taste by his own time—I should be glad if I could be sure that I or any critic to-day was as catholic in taste, or had such justification for his limitations. It would seem nowadays a futile pastime, for instance, to turn Chaucer into modern English. But for Dryden's time it was no more futile than it would be considered nowadays to paraphrase such a thing as *Gawain and the Green Knight*, or even Anglo-Saxon. For one point, Chaucer was then a neglected and unappreciated author; Dryden was not, any more than most of his contemporaries, a scholarly student of middle English; and it shows great perceptiveness on his part to have recognised Chaucer and praised him as he did. Furthermore, Dryden could not consider the English language, as we very foolishly and lazily are inclined to do, as *The* finished and complete; he was in the thick of *Critic* the struggle to modernise it. We must keep in mind this latter point, when we read his strictures upon the Elizabethans, and especially upon Shakespeare. Possibly, in retrospect, we are right in thinking that he somewhat exaggerates the worth of Fletcher, relative to Shakespeare. But take his comments upon Shakespeare one by one, and you will find, I believe, that most of them are just. We are so habituated to considering Shakespeare above criticism, that we cannot admit that Dryden's praise of Shakespeare is as high praise as our own; and that if we stop to apprehend the values which were rightly important for Dryden in his time, his occasional censure of Shakespeare is usually right.

It is natural that, with the French theory and practice in view, and with the imperfect knowledge of the Greek theatre, and of the meaning of Aristotle's comments upon it, current at the *57* time, Dryden should often have gone wrong in *John* his dramatic criticism. Owing to thus abusing *Dryden* the sense of Aristotle's *Poetics*, many men have erred in trying to erect a final theory of what the theatre ought to be and must be from what it has been. We must not look to Dryden's theories for the genesis of Dryden's practice in the theatre; rather, we find a theory which is a compromise between Aristotle, as he understood Aristotle through distorting French lenses, and his own practice which is itself a compromise between earlier English practice and French practice. Much, for which he appeals to authority, is merely, in his own practice, the result of a sense of form and order working against the disorderliness of the Elizabethan stage. And it must be admitted that the Elizabethans neglected certain very positive dramatic virtues. We are accustomed, and rightly, to look to Shakespeare for more than dramatic virtues, for a "pattern" of feeling that Dryden could not see, 58 because Dryden was not looking for it but for something else; and therefore some of Dryden's criticisms of Shakespeare's later plays appear to us supercilious and shallow. But Shakespeare could play his own mighty music upon any instruments that came to hand; and he was not concerned, consciously, greatly to alter the form which he found ready. But Dryden's common sense, and sense of order, were imperative to him; and we must take his theory largely as a kind of legal justification for what he felt was right.

Dryden first, following the French, misunderstands the Aristotelian theory of the Unities of Time and Place; and then, disapproving of the French strictness (he is a good patriot, and never fails to speak up for English drama against French when the occasion offers), proceeds to qualify it. For instance, he reprehends the attempt to condense the history of twenty-four years into a representation of three hours (one would like to read his critique of *Back to Methuselah*), but approves the representation of

twenty-four hours in the same space. What is
true is, I think, in practice, that more *unity of poetic feeling* (which is the only unity that matters) can be obtained *as a rule*, with a minimum of difference between times and places. I say *as a rule*, for some actions obviously cannot be represented at all without making great leaps of time or space. Dryden's view, as it stands, is literally absurd; for it would make *Coriolanus* a better play than *Antony and Cleopatra*, solely for the reason that the distance from Rome to Antium is shorter than that from Rome to Egypt. But the rigidity of Dryden's theory must not blind us to the accuracy of Dryden's common sense.

Here and there Dryden goes wrong in ways which it is less easy to pardon. For instance, he speaks of the comic element in Elizabethan tragedy as being employed for what we call "comic relief." No doubt, from the point of view of dramatic effect, this comic element was, for the great majority of the Elizabethan audience, comic *relief.* "Laughter and tears" are still advertised as attractions to some film or other; and doubtless the Elizabethans liked to sandwich their laughter and tears as much as modern audiences do. But a very little examination of Elizabethan drama, and especially of Shakespeare, will convince us that the comic is not really "relief" at all, but on the contrary, at its best an intensification of the sombreness. The Porter in *Macbeth*, the Gravedigger in *Hamlet*, the Fool in *Lear*, the drunkenness of Lepidus in *Antony and Cleopatra*—there is no "relief" in these; they merely make the horror or tragedy more real by transposing it for a moment from the sublime to the common. But we were wrong if we expected Dryden to perceive this; for it is just the sort of thing he would not have perceived.

Dryden was not only the first great English poet to set down carefully his theories about the practice of his own art, but he is also, allowing for the limitations of his age, what we may

The
Critic

call the *normal* critic. Johnson, in his *Lives of* *the Poets*, adopts a more particular method; his general views of the nature of poetry, and regulations of the art, occur here and there during the course of biographical critiques of particular poets; Dryden is directly concerned with the proper art of poetry, and his remarks on particular poets occur only as illustrations. Coleridge, in his great disorderly book of criticism, is no safe model for other reasons than mere disorder, for he does not restrain himself to criticism, but runs into philosophy and æsthetics. Wordsworth is occupied, in his fine prefaces to the *Lyrical Ballads* with defending his own practices, and is not accordingly a model for normal criticisms of poetry; and Matthew Arnold is too largely concerned with finding the moral lesson. Dryden is concerned neither with appreciation nor with æsthetics. He was fortunate in his age, when philosophical writing was practised in England with a language which

had just been developed to the point of expressing adequately abstract ideas, and before writing about poetry had come to mean philoso- phising about it. It is also fortunate for us to have had a critic who wrote so well and with such authority about poetry, at a time when neither the fundamental nature of the poetic activity nor the social function of poetry was yet considered the subject matter of literary criticism. As testimony of the clarity of Dryden's expression and the just sobriety of his theory, I mention an essay called *The Proper Wit of Poetry*, and particularly the third paragraph, in which he defines Wit. It will be observed that it does not occur to Dryden to distinguish to the point of isolation the reasoning from the imaginative faculty; it would not have occurred to him that there was or should be anything *irrational* in poetic imagination. He says:

"*The first happiness of the poet's imagination is properly invention, or finding of the thought; the second is fancy, or the variation, deriving or mould-*

*ing of that thought, as the judgment represents it
proper to the subject; the third is elocution, or the
art of clothing and adorning that thought so found
and varied in apt, significant and sounding words:
the quickness of the imagination is seen in the invention, the fertility in the fancy and the accuracy
in the expression."*

The distinction between thought and image,
and the distinction between the thought and the
clothing of it in elocution, are foreign to modern
theory of poetry; but I think that these distinc-
tions are safer than many that more recent writers
have made; and the part of inspiration (or free
association) and the part of conscious labour
are justly kept in place.

A great merit of Dryden as a critic and as a
critical influence is that he never transgresses the
line beyond which the criticisms of poetry become something else. In that happy age it did
not occur to him to enquire what poetry was
for, how it affected the nerves of listeners, how

it sublimated the wishes of the poet, whom it should satisfy, and all the other questions which really have nothing to do with poetry as poetry; and the poet was not expected to be either a sibyl or a prophet. The purpose of poetry and drama was to *amuse*; but it was to amuse properly; and the larger forms of poetry should have a moral significance; by exhibiting the thoughts and passions of man through lively image and melodious verse, to edify and to refine the reader and auditor.

I do not know that we have improved upon this conception of the place and function of poetry. I do not pretend that Dryden as a critic is often profound, any more than I make that claim for him as a poet; but the more I consider contemporary reflexion upon poetry, the more thankful I am for what we may call Dryden's critical orthodoxy. In his opinions there is no extravagance. Now it seems to me that there is a very widespread tendency, which takes various forms nowadays, to treat poetry as a kind of religion or substitute for religion. The germ, or something more developed than the germ, of this way of thinking is to be found in the criticism of Matthew Arnold, who is to that extent an heresiarch. Arnold dismisses altogether the intellectual element in religion, and leaves only art and morals; art, and particularly literary art, inculcates morals, and truly moral art is all that Arnold leaves us in the place of religious faith. It is only a short step, if any step be necessary, to finding in literature the satisfaction which we deny ourselves in religion. This new confusion takes several forms. I find it in the humanism of Irving Babbitt, and in the more recent theories of critics of such opposed views as Middleton Murry and I. A. Richards. Mr. Murry seems to maintain that poetry *is* religion; Mr. Richards rather more moderately that poetry is the best thing we can have nowadays instead of religion. I am not concerned to criticise such theories from a theological point of view; for indeed they fall beyond the reach of such criticism; I

John Dryden

66

am anxious rather lest they distort our enjoy-
ment of poetry. The poet tends to be appointed,
not indeed a priest of his own cult, for he is
not allowed to interpret himself; but rather a
Grand Llama imprisoned in princely privacy
while the critical priests carry on the real business. A dead poet for this purpose is better than
a living one, as he cannot be so indiscreet as to
speak for himself. But criticism itself will be
biassed, according to the particular oracles we
consult; and as some critics will find their religion in some poetry and others in others, the
judgment of poetry as poetry will become of
dwindling interest.

Dryden, then, both as poet and as critic, seems
to me a very great defender of sanity. I do not
think that I have made any extravagant claims
for him. For that matter, I have not said much
that is original. Dryden is no discovery; there
are few of his merits as a writer that have not
been discovered and brought to light by one or
another earlier critic. I have no desire to see his

works on every drawing room table, or even to *John* see a generation of versifiers employ their talent *Dryden* upon political satire and theological controversy. I do not suppose that at any time he will ever be anyone's favourite poet, or engross the adolescent mind for a season as the romantic poets can do. I have purposely avoided trying to give a course in "How to Enjoy Dryden," because the people who can really enjoy his poetry need no assistance from me or from anyone. But it is worth while to know what Dryden did for the English language in verse and in prose, because we shall understand better what the language is, and of what it is still capable.